Armand Bombardier

Inventor of the Snowmobile

EDITORIAL DEVELOPMENT BY MICHAEL WEBB

Copp Clark Pitman Ltd.
A Longman Company

ISBN 0-7730-5051-5 (Casebound)   ISBN 0-7730-5052-3 (Paperback)

Canadian Cataloguing in Publication Data
Main entry under title:
Armand Bombardier, inventor of the snowmobile

(Scientists & inventors series)
ISBN 0-7730-5051-5 (bound)   ISBN 0-7730-5052-3 (pbk.)

1. Bombardier, Joseph-Armand, 1907–1964 — Juvenile literature. 2. Snowmobiles — Quebec (Province) — History — Juvenile literature. 3. Inventors — Quebec (Province) — Biography — Juvenile literature. I. Webb, Michael, 1949–   . II. Series.

TL140.B65A75 1991   j629.22'042'092   C90-095372-1

MICHAEL WEBB, a former school teacher and chemistry professor, now works as an editor and writer in Toronto. He has a doctorate in chemistry from the University of Alberta.

RESEARCH: *Jo Mrozewski*
EDITING AND PHOTO RESEARCH: *Grace D'Alfonso*
DESIGN AND ART DIRECTION: *Susan Hedley*
TYPESETTING: *Sonja Mills Graphic Arts Inc.*
PRINTING AND BINDING: *Friesen Printers Ltd.*

ACKNOWLEDGEMENTS
Many thanks to Mary Louise Standish of the J.A. Bombardier Museum for commenting on the manuscript. Also, special thanks to Francesca Verre, aged 11, for reading the manuscript.

PHOTO AND ILLUSTRATION CREDITS
Bombardier Inc.: 18, 22, 23, 24, 25; *J.A. Bombardier Museum:* cover, iv, 2, 5, 6, 7, 9, 11, 12, 14, 15, 17, 21; *Malcolm Cullen:* 8; *Miller Comstock:* 3, 4, 10, 13, 16, 19; *National Archives of Canada:* 1; *University of Sherbrooke:* 20.

Copp Clark Pitman Ltd., 2775 Matheson Blvd. East,
Mississauga, Ontario L4W 4P7

Printed and bound in Canada.

CONTENTS

Armand Bombardier in his factory.

It's hard to think of Canada without thinking of snow. There is a good side to snow, which we use in many winter sports, such as skiing and snowmobiling. Snow also brings some problems, such as clogged streets. But today, snow can be cleared quickly, so that people can get on with their lives.

But imagine the days before snowplows and snowblowers. How did people get to school or go to work? How could they get medical help in an emergency? There were not many choices. They might be lucky and live close to a busy road, on which snow would get packed down. Then they might use a horse and sleigh. Otherwise, they might choose to put on snowshoes or hitch up a dog team.

A man putting on his snowshoes.

*Young Armand, dressed up for a special
church event.*

The Canadian who did most to overcome the problems that snow
caused was Armand Bombardier. It was already clear when he was
a boy that he was a gifted inventor.

He was born on April 16, 1907, in Valcourt, Québec. His
parents, who farmed near Valcourt, named him Joseph-Armand.
They called him Armand for short. He was the oldest of eight
children.

Even as a young boy, Armand began to tinker with machines. By the age of ten, he was helping out in the woodworking shop on the farm. Soon after, he started to fix broken engines in cars and farm machinery. By the age of 15, he was a very good **mechanic**. He was the person to call when a machine broke down.

By then, he was living in the village of Valcourt, where his parents had bought the general store when he was 13. Because farm life was hard, they wanted their children to have other choices.

Young Armand was pleased with the move. With fewer chores to do than on the farm, he had more time for his inventing. Also, he could get paid for making deliveries from the store and for helping the local priest at Mass on Sundays.

A mechanic fixing an engine.

Armand spent his money at the local jewellery store on springs and other parts of watches. He used these bits and pieces to build toy tractors, trains, and motorboats.

When he was 14, Armand was given a broken pistol by Dr. Archambault, the local veterinarian. Armand made it into a small cannon, which worked when loaded with gunpowder. Neither Dr. Archambault nor Armand's father was happy about this dangerous invention.

The inside of a watch.

Armand built this toy tractor.

Armand had spent his first year in Valcourt studying at the village school. But, at 14, he was sent away to the St-Charles-Borromée Seminary in Sherbrooke. His parents wanted him to be a priest. Though Armand was very religious and stayed a loyal Roman Catholic all his life, he wanted to be a mechanic.

When only 15, Armand began what was to be his most important work. He built his first snowmobile! To stop Armand from experimenting on the family car, his father had given him an old car. Over the Christmas holidays, Armand mounted the car's engine on four sleigh runners. He also made a wooden propellor, which he fixed to the back of the engine.

Armand and his brother Léopold tested the new machine. It made a tremendous noise because Armand could not find a suitable **muffler**. The machine ran well for over a kilometre. But their father thought that the machine was a danger to drive. He was furious and ordered the boys to take it apart. But, by then, Armand knew he could build a snowmobile that worked.

Armand's first snowmobile.

After two years at the Seminary, Armand got his way. He started as an **apprentice** mechanic at the Gosselin Garage in South Stukely. He soon needed more training and left for Montréal. There, he worked as a mechanic during the day and took **correspondence courses** to study mechanics and electricity at night.

In May, 1926, at age 19, Armand returned to Valcourt. His father bought a piece of land in the village and built a garage for his son to work in. Armand sold and repaired cars. He also repaired engines used by local farmers in their machinery.

His business, *Garage Bombardier*, was a success, so Armand was very busy. Even with three employees, he worked up to fourteen hours a day six days a week. He liked to be involved in everything — he was still the chief mechanic, as well as selling cars. He even took an **accounting** course, so that he could run his business properly.

Part of Garage Bombardier *as it now appears at the J. Armand Bombardier Museum.*

Armand was very happy with his job, though it left him little time to relax. He sang in the church choir and liked swimming, hunting, and fishing. He also liked to drive cars, often very fast. And, of course, he liked to build snowmobiles.

His early attempts were cars with extra wheels added at the back. Chains or belts around the wheels helped them grip the snow. He replaced the front wheels with runners that looked like skis. Some of his designs worked well. Others would break down on test drives, leaving him to walk back to town.

Armand changed a Model T Ford car into a snowmobile.

Armand and Yvonne on their wedding day.

Then Armand began to date Yvonne Labrecque, the sister of one of his employees. Armand and Yvonne were married on August 7, 1929. That same year, Armand, at age 22, was able to buy the garage from his father. The next few years were difficult because the Bombardiers soon had a young family to support.

For five years, they lived in an apartment above a store. They had no running water or electricity. The first two of their six children were born there. Both were sons, Germain and Yvon.

A Terrible Event

In January, 1934, two-year old Yvon suddenly became very ill. The doctor, suspecting **appendicitis**, had to get the child to a hospital. But the nearest one was in Sherbrooke, about 50 kilometres away. The roads were blocked with snow, and Armand did not have a snowmobile in working order. The young boy died within hours of becoming ill. This terrible event was an example of how important snowmobiles could be.

After his son's death, Armand carried on building different models of snowmobiles. Some of the early machines were successful enough to be sold in small numbers. Fearing that others would copy his ideas, Armand applied to **patent** them. His first patent was issued on June 29, 1937. It protected his invention for 17 years. Anyone who used it during that time had to pay Armand.

Even today, snow sometimes makes travel difficult.

By the time he got the patent, Armand had designed his first popular snowmobile. It was called the B7 (B for Bombardier; 7 because it could carry 7 people). He quickly sold 20 B7s, mostly to doctors and funeral directors. Then Armand changed the machine a little and sold another 50, mostly to people who delivered milk and to travelling salespeople.

Armand standing behind a B7.

The B12.

With this success, Armand stopped repairing cars and worked full-time on snowmobiles. He changed the name of his business from *Garage Bombardier* to *L'Auto-Neige Bombardier*, which means "Bombardier Snowmobile."

With more improvements, about 100 B7s were sold in 1938. The future looked bright. But, on September 3, 1939, came the start of **World War II** in Europe. A week later, Canada joined the War.

In the six war years, the Canadian Government would not let Armand sell very many B7s or the new and larger B12s. He could only sell to people with special permits. *L'Auto-Neige Bombardier* spent the war years building **troop carriers** for the Government.

When the War ended, the Québec Government created another problem for Armand. It passed a law requiring that roads be plowed to keep them open in winter. So people would be able to use their regular cars, rather than needing a "snow car" like the B7.

A modern snowplow at work.

Armand had just developed a large snowmobile bus, the C18, which could carry 25 children to school. Sales of his snowmobiles were good until 1947. But Armand knew that, with more and more roads being kept open in winter, his market would soon shrink. He had better dream up something new. So he travelled across Canada to get ideas.

A C18 being used as a school bus.

A Muskeg Tractor in use.

He watched lumberjacks at work. When logs were cut, they were slowly dragged from the forest by horsedrawn sled. So, in 1949, Armand changed the B12 to make the BT. This machine had only a small cabin at the front and a large platform to carry wood.

In Alberta, Armand watched oil workers struggle through swampy land called **muskeg**. He later designed a mobile **drilling platform** for use on this kind of land. And, by 1953, he completed one of his greatest inventions, the Muskeg Tractor.

The idea had been to build a machine for oil companies in Canada. But the Muskeg Tractor was used worldwide. It even plowed sand from roads in the Sahara Desert and carried people across Antarctica! But Armand Bombardier's most famous invention was yet to come.

The sales of his machines and the money he made from his patents made Armand a very rich man. But his life changed very little. He still worked long hours and kept on inventing.

Since he had first thought about snowmobiles, he had dreamt of inventing a machine that could carry one or two people through deep snow. In 1957, he set to work. At first, he thought the machine should be like a car, but he soon knew that it should be more like a motorcycle. He called his new invention the Ski-Dog, because he wanted it to replace a dog team.

Armand hoped the Ski-Dog would replace dog teams.

Armand test driving a Ski-Dog.

Armand by now owned a large factory. His workers set about making Ski-Dogs. But the name was soon changed to Ski-Doo, which sounded better. The first 225 of them were sold in 1959. Armand had thought of trappers in the Canadian North as his obvious market. But many groups, including farmers and the police, began to use the Ski-Doo.

THE SKI-DOO

Today, the Ski-Doo is very important in cold regions, like Northern Canada. Doctors, police, trappers, oil workers, and miners often depend on Ski-Doos. This situation would probably not have surprised Armand Bombardier. After all, he designed the Ski-Doo to work more quickly and more cheaply than a dog team.

It did surprise Armand when people started to use the Ski-Doo for fun. Armand himself became a keen Ski-Doo racer.

A Ski-Doo racer.

Like many new inventions, the Ski-Doo had its problems. Some people thought that it was too noisy, damaged the **environment**, and had too many accidents. Yet snowmobiling is still a popular sport. Some machines are driven in races, but most are used as a way to enjoy the outdoors in winter.

The sales of Ski-Doos show how popular they are. The Bombardier company is not the only one making this type of snowmobile today. But this company alone has sold well over two million (2 000 000) of them! North America has around 10 000 snowmobile clubs, which give people with snowmobiles the chance to get together.

Enjoying the outdoors by snowmobile.

As the inventor of many famous machines, Armand became well-known. He was highly respected, especially in Québec. To recognize his work, the University of Sherbrooke named one of its buildings after him.

Sadly, soon after his Ski-Doo became such a success, Armand's health began to fail. In November, 1963, he had two operations for stomach cancer, but nothing more could be done. He had only a few weeks to live.

This building at the University of Sherbrooke is named after J. Armand Bombardier.

The office of the Garage Bombardier *as it now appears at the J. Armand Bombardier Museum.*

Among the last things he did was to plan a **charitable foundation**. Its offices are on a street named after him in Valcourt. The foundation's work includes the funding of sports and other activities in the Valcourt area. It also supports the work of **missionaries** outside Canada and helps bright students go to university.

Armand Bombardier died on February 18, 1964, at the age of 56. If you are ever in Valcourt, you can visit the J. Armand Bombardier Museum to see an exhibition of his work.

But the Bombardier story does not end there. At the time of his death, Armand Bombardier could not have imagined how his company would grow. Even the 6000 orders for Ski-Doos in 1963 could not have given him much idea.

BOMBARDIER INC.

Other Bombardier family members took over the company, which then had 380 workers, most of them in Valcourt. By 1990, Bombardier Inc. was a **multinational corporation**. There were 22 500 employees in various countries, including Canada, the United States, France, Belgium, Austria, and the United Kingdom.

You will see Bombardier products almost everywhere you go. The company builds railway cars for several types of trains, including subway trains. It now owns the North American rights to the French high speed train. This can travel at up to 300 kilometres per hour. Bombardier Inc. wants to build high speed train routes in North America.

The overhead monorail at Walt Disney World in Florida is a Bombardier train.

An executive jet built by Canadair.

A very different kind of Bombardier train is the overhead monorail at Walt Disney World in Florida. In 1989, Bombardier won a contract to build railway cars for the tunnel that will connect England and France under the English Channel.

The company has expanded into the **aerospace industry**. It owns aircraft companies, including Canadair and Learjet Corporation. Both these companies build **executive jets**. Canadair also builds larger passenger aircraft. Another kind of Canadair plane is a water bomber, which drops water on forest fires.

A Canadair water bomber.

The military work begun by Armand in World War II has also grown. Canadair builds **spy rockets**. A company owned by Bombardier in Northern Ireland builds military aircraft and missiles.

There are too many other Bombardier products to list. They include engines for **ultralight aircraft**. The Sea-Doo, a type of Ski-Doo that travels across water, is very popular. Even the Apollo space missions that landed astronauts on the moon used Bombardier parts in **lunar modules**.

The company has not forgotten the importance of snow to its business. Bombardier machines have been used to prepare ski slopes, such as those for the Winter Olympics. And, of course, the Bombardier company is still the world's largest producer of snowmobiles!

This business empire has grown quickly from the work begun by a brilliant mechanic with an inventive mind and good business sense. It has all come about because Armand Bombardier chose to devote his life to making the Canadian winter easier to deal with.

Sea-Doos.

GLOSSARY

accounting — A way to keep track of the money a person or business makes and spends. *(p. 7)*

aerospace industry — The companies that build planes, rockets, spacecraft, and other machines to carry goods or people through the air or into space. *(p. 23)*

appendicitis — A painful condition of a small part of the body called the appendix. *(p. 10)*

apprentice — A person who learns to do a job by working with someone who is already good at it. (An apprentice carpenter learns by working with a carpenter.) *(p. 7)*

charitable foundation — An organization that spends its money on helping people and does not make any profit. *(p. 21)*

correspondence courses — Series of lessons run by mail, not in a classroom. Students get material by mail, do their work, and mail it in. *(p. 7)*

drilling platform — A flat surface that supports a drill used to make holes in the ground. Drilling platforms are often used to find oil. *(p. 15)*

environment — Everything that surrounds and affects living things. *(p. 19)*

executive jets — Small planes that carry business people quickly from one place to another for meetings. *(p. 23)*

lunar modules — Small spacecraft that carry astronauts onto the surface of the moon. *(p. 24)*

mechanic — A person who repairs machines. *(p. 3)*

missionaries — People who spread their religion to others. Some missionaries also help people in need, such as the poor and hungry. *(p. 21)*

muffler — Something fixed to an engine so that it makes less noise. *(p. 6)*

multinational corporation — A large company with branches in different countries. *(p. 22)*

muskeg — Soft, very wet land. It is often covered with lots of dead plants under water. *(p. 15)*

patent — A way you can register an invention or discovery, so that you are the only person with the right to make or sell it for a certain number of years. *(p. 10)*

spy rockets — Types of rockets that carry cameras and other tools that observe the Earth from above to get information. *(p. 24)*

troop carriers — Machines that carry soldiers from one place to another. *(p. 12)*

ultralight aircraft — A very small plane in which the pilot sits in the open. There are usually three wheels, and the engine and propellor are behind the pilot's head. *(p. 24)*

World War II — The war from 1939 to 1945. It started with Germany and Italy against the United Kingdom and other countries, including Canada. Many other countries joined the War later. *(p. 12)*

1 2 3 4 5 5051-5 95 94 93 92 91

1 2 3 4 5 5052-3 95 94 93 92 91